FABULOUS FORWARDS

Marty Nabhan

BASKETBALL
HEROES

The Rourke Corporation, Inc.
Vero Beach, Florida 32964

The Rourke Corporation, Inc.
P.O. Box 3328, Vero Beach, FL 32964

Nabhan, Marty.
      Fabulous forwards / by Marty Nabhan.
            p.   cm. — (Basketball heroes)
      Includes bibliographical references (p. 47) and index.
      Summary: Discusses the role of the forward in professional basketball and describes some of the game's best, including Larry Bird, Julius Erving, and Karl Malone.
      ISBN 0-86593-161-5
      1. Basketball—United States—Offense—Juvenile literature.   2. Forwards (Basketball)—United States—Biography—Juvenile literature. [1. Forwards (Basketball) 2. Basketball.]
      I. Title. II. Series.
      GV889.N334   1992   92-9479
      796.323'0973—dc20   CIP
                                                              AC

Series Editor: Gregory Lee
Editor: Marguerite Aronowitz
Book design and production: The Creative Spark, San Clemente, CA
Cover photograph: Mike Powell/ALLSPORT

Contents

Throughout the 1980s, the best forward in the NBA was Larry Bird, a Celtics favorite and future Hall of Famer.

The Bird Takes Flight

He just doesn't look like a basketball player. He looks more like a farmer—a "good ol' boy" who is going to compete in the local tractor pull. But on the court, Larry Bird, the six-foot, nine-inch forward for the Boston Celtics, looks like one of the greatest players in the history of the game. The Celtics are always a threat to win as long as Bird is on the floor. And that's precisely where he ends up sometimes: on the floor. Like in the 1991 playoff game against the Indiana Pacers. Bird took a spill and landed on his face on the hardwood court. Shaken, he left the game. But when he came back in, he led the Celts to victory.

"The number one thing is desire," Bird said. "The ability to do the things you have to do to become a basketball player. I don't think you can teach anyone desire. I think it's a gift. I don't know why I have it, but I do."

Throughout the 1980s, Bird and Los Angeles Lakers' guard Magic Johnson battled for the right to be called number one. They played against each other in the college basketball finals of 1979, Bird with Indiana State and Johnson with Michigan State. Later that year they both began their careers in the NBA. They would dominate the game for the next decade. Between them, their teams won eight of a possible ten championships in the 1980s, facing each other for three of them.

Bird comes from French Lick, Indiana. While at

Indiana State he led his team to 33 straight victories. He was drafted by the Celtics while still in his junior year of college. The Celtics won only 29 games the year before he came. In his first pro year, Bird turned the Celtics' fortunes around. They went from 29 wins to 61, and the best record in the NBA. Bird was named Rookie of the Year, and he was just getting started.

The Celtics have made the playoffs every year with Bird as their forward. They played in the finals five times, winning three of them. Bird was named Most Valuable Player in the regular season three years in a row, from 1984 to 1986. He won the playoff MVP award twice. Add to these triumphs Bird's victories in the NBA three-point shoot-out contests at All-Star games, and you have enough trophies to fill a small museum.

But Bird's career has not been about trophies. It's been about team play. Few players in league history can shoot, pass, and rebound the ball as well as Bird. He has an uncanny ability to find an open man and get the ball to him, often without looking. And if his team is behind with

Bird says that hard work and desire helped him become one of the league's all-time great players.

only seconds to play, Bird is the player to make the winning shot.

Hard Work And Timing

The memory of the Celtics on the ropes is still vivid. They were ready to lose the 1987 playoffs to the Detroit Pistons, trailing with only a few seconds left to play. All Piston Isiah Thomas had to do was inbound the ball. He threw it quickly to a teammate, but Bird stepped in front of it, stealing the ball. He tossed it to teammate Dennis Johnson for the lay-up, and the Celtics were winners.

What impresses so many experts is that Bird seems to have little physical talent. But what he lacks in natural ability, he makes up for with great feeling for the game.

"I would say my vision, my court awareness, and my height are God-given," Bird said. "Everything else I've worked my butt off for." Bird's reputation as a hard worker has earned him the respect of nearly everyone in the NBA.

Injuries have slowed Bird down since the mid-1980s. First his elbow, then his legs, and now his back have given him problems. Still, he continues to fight, continues to work, continues to win. And if the game is on the line, there's no doubt about it: The Celtics' hopes will be in the hands of Larry Bird.

The forward must play a tough, contact game in order to get the shots he wants—or slow the offense of someone like Charles Barkley.

Basketball's Hot Hands

Think about the description of Superman. He is "faster than a speeding bullet." He is "more powerful than a locomotive." And he is "able to leap tall buildings in a single bound." The same may be said of forwards in the NBA. They have speed, power, and leaping ability that seems almost superhuman.

Each team usually puts two forwards in a game at one time. These men are often taller than guards and shorter than centers. But because of the position they play on the court, they need the talents of both guards and centers. No other players on the court have quite the same role as those that play the forward position.

The forward on offense covers a lot of the court. He plays from the outside corners to the area under the basket. He may try to shoot from a distance, or he might try spinning around a center for a lay-up in

---

Forward Trivia

Q: Michael Jordan set the NBA record for most points in a playoff game with 63. But that game went into double overtime. What forward holds the record for points scored in a regulation playoff game?
A: Elgin Baylor of the Los Angeles Lakers, with 61 points against the Boston Celtics, April 14, 1962.

Q: Who was a star forward in the American Basketball Association before joining the NBA and leading the 76ers to three championship appearances and one title?
A: Julius Erving. "Dr. J" led the 76ers to the Finals in 1980 and 1982, and won it all in 1983.

the middle of the key in front of the basket. On defense, he can guard his man wherever he goes, or double-team the opposing center.

These NBA supermen need speed, physical size, leaping ability, and strength. Each one of these skills helps a forward play well. Speed helps the forward perform from one end of the court to the other. He can fly down the court on a fast break. He can run back on defense to keep the other team from scoring. His speed helps him guard his man away from the basket. And if an opponent gets by a teammate, a quick forward can switch to guard that opponent.

Since the forward often plays near the basket, his height comes in handy. He can block shots, rebound, and score over defenders. If he is tall and wide, he can take up more room. He can set *screens*, blocking a teammate's defender so the teammate is free to score. Also, the larger forward puts himself between his opponent and the basket. This is called *boxing out*, or keeping the opponent from getting rebounds by staying in his way.

Leaping ability also aids the forward. The higher he can jump, the better chance he has of getting rebounds away from taller men. Fowards that know how to keep good position and jump high often get more rebounds than centers. Some forwards use leaping ability to soar through the air and make amazing shots.

The last key to a forward's success is strength. Although basketball is called a non-contact sport, it can be a bruising game. A lot of pushing and shoving occurs under the basket. A forward has to fight for position. He pushes to get near the basket. He leans on opponents to keep them away. What he sometimes lacks in size, he makes up for with strength and grit. Some of the roughest, toughest players in the NBA are forwards.

Brutal Beginnings

When Dr. James Naismith invented basketball in 1891, he wanted to make it a non-violent game. He studied violent sports and determined that because players could run with the ball, the games were more dangerous. In rugby and football, players who ran with the ball were tackled. This would be dangerous on hard wooden floors, so he made it a rule that players had to pass the ball to move it.

Still, the early game got rough. It was first played by Dr. Naismith's rowdy gym class at the YMCA. Restless players, hoping for an indoor game that was as fast and exciting as rough outdoor sports, got their wish. They liked the game immediately. Although there was no tackling, there was plenty of wrestling and struggling for the ball.

If the ball went out of bounds, the first team to get to it put it back into play. This led to players running over each other as well as the fans. To keep the ball on the court, teams began playing behind a wire fence called a cage. In the early days, in fact, players were known as "cagers." The cage became a part of the game, and players got good at bouncing the ball off the cage to teammates down court.

Even with the cage, however, the game was still violent. Many players would be shoved against it and came away with scrapes and cage marks on their bodies. Changing the cage to rope netting didn't help. Joel Gotthoffer, a star from the 1930s, said, "I played the first few games in a [rope] cage, and I came home with the cage's markings on me. You could play tic-tac-toe on everybody after a game because the cage marked you up. Sometimes you were bleeding and sometimes not. You were like a gladiator. And if you didn't get rid of the ball, you could get killed."

Cages were soon eliminated, and the game was

*In his Hall of Fame career forward Bob Pettit scored 20,880
points and averaged 26.4 points per game.*

changed to make it less dangerous. Although it could still be rough, the emphasis was on skill rather than brute strength. And one of the earliest players to show this skill was forward Bob Pettit.

Pettit was clumsy as a youth. He didn't make his high school team until he was a junior. But his hard work and determination paid off. Pettit became one of the smoothest players on the court. He came to the St. Louis Hawks in 1954, where he perfected his scoring and rebounding abilities. In 1958, he led the Hawks to their only world championship.

A San Francisco Scorer

The 1960s and 1970s saw the rise of more star forwards. Rick Barry broke in with the San Francisco Warriors in 1965. The six-foot, seven-inch star was a master scorer. In just his second season with the Warriors, Barry led the league in scoring with a 35.6 points-per-game average. But it was from the free-throw line where Barry was most deadly. He had an unusual style, shooting his free throws underhand. But his twirling shot went in 90 percent of the time.

Elgin Baylor of the Los Angeles Lakers was another super-scoring forward. He was often called the most graceful man on the court as he moved his six-foot, five-inch frame around players as though he were a ballet dancer. His single-game scoring high was 71 points. In the 1961-62 season, Baylor set a single-season scoring record for forwards, averaging 38.3 points a game.

John "Hondo" Havlicek of the Boston Celtics was a double threat. In his 16-year career, he racked up more than 26,000 points on offense. But his defense was just as feared. The six-foot, five-inch Havlicek often stole the ball at key moments, helping the Celtics win the game. He was on six championship teams.

Philadelphia's Julius Erving (6) was a graceful player and the third-highest point scorer of all time. Here he works against Rick Barry, a Hall of Fame forward with more than 25,000 points in his career.

But for sheer glamor and superstar status, Julius Erving was perhaps in a league of his own. Erving starred for years in the American Basketball Association (ABA) for the New Jersey Nets. "Doctor J" entered the NBA in 1976 with the Philadelphia 76ers, and showed many new fans why he was so good. Erving could score from anywhere. His fly-through-the-air antics left defenders scratching their heads, wondering just how he did it. But fly he did, scoring more than any forward in league history. His 30,026 career points are third just after centers Kareem Abdul-Jabbar and Wilt Chamberlain.

Today's Forward

Erving retired in 1987, having set the stage for today's forward. The 1980s saw many changes in the position. Larry Bird of the Celtics showed that a forward could be just as important to his team as a guard or center.

At seven-foot, four-inches, Ralph Sampson of the Houston Rockets showed that a forward could be taller than the center and still get the job done. Sampson started his career as a center. Later he played forward next to Hakeem Olajuwon. The duo was known as the "Twin Towers." Many teams have since had their version of the Twin Towers, featuring a tall forward who could bully with the best.

Today there are as many types of forwards as there are players. Some specialize in scoring. Some take more rebounds. The forward's duties are now divided into two categories. There is the smaller, more mobile forward, called the *small forward*, who is able to score and pass at will. And there is the stronger, bigger forward, called the *power forward*, who can power the ball to the hoop and muscle with the big men.

On some teams the difference between the two is clear. On other teams, the differences are less obvious. Dennis Rodman, for example, is often listed as a small forward.

Yet Rodman is one of the best rebounders in basketball. Karl Malone at power forward gets more assists than his team's small forward. Small forward Charles Barkley plays as physically as any power forward.

*The great Elgin Baylor has the third-highest scoring average in
NBA history (27.4), behind Michael Jordan and Wilt Chamberlain.*

Generally, the small forward is the most likely to have good ball-handling skills. He can shoot from the inside, but likes the outside shot. He is more likely to pass the ball than the power forward, and will often have more assists. The power forward is often stronger and taller than the small forward. He plays nearer the basket and is involved in more physical play. He takes his shots at close range and will usually shoot a high percentage. He is a good rebounder, often getting more rebounds than his team's center.

Either forward can dominate a game in many ways. In the 1990-91 NBA season, three of the top four scorers were forwards. Three of the top four rebounders were forwards. Three of the top four players in field goal percentage were forwards. Whether he uses force or finesse, the forward is a pivotal and critical part of today's NBA team.

One of the NBA's most versatile scorers is Scottie Pippen, a key factor in the Chicago Bull's championship victory in 1991.

Pivots, Picks, And Posting Up

The forward leans back against his man, facing away from the basket. He waves to a teammate, signalling he's ready for the ball. The teammate passes the ball. But the opponent continues to push the forward's back. He is determined not to let the forward get closer to the hoop.

The forward dribbles the ball. He feels that his defender is leaning more on his right side. Using his left arm as a shield, the forward spins on his left foot away from his opponent, then leaps for the basket. There is just one obstacle between him and scoring two points: the long arm of the seven-foot center.

He fakes the shot. While still in mid-air, he brings the ball back down. He continues to soar under the basket. Using the rim as a shield against the center's outstretched arm, the forward twirls the ball up against the backboard. If the spin is just right, the ball falls through the hoop for the score.

Posting up with the pivot move is not new in basketball. It originated in the early days of basketball. In the late 1800s, Dr. Naismith's new game was being played in many YMCA buildings on hardwood gym floors. But many of the YMCA leaders thought the game was too rough and didn't want it played in their buildings. Players looked elsewhere for places to play, but the only buildings large enough were skating rinks, barns, and dance halls.

In some makeshift arenas, posts and pillars used to support the roof dotted the floor and presented players with new obstacles. Rather than complain, however, the players used them to their advantage. For example, if an opponent tried to steal the ball, the offensive player could dribble behind the post and use it as a shield. Some clever ball handlers ran for the post while a defender guarded them closely. When the ball handler ran by the post, it acted like a screen—practically knocking the defender down.

"Post play" became common in basketball. Before too long, players realized that they could do the same thing by using their bodies. By standing in just the right spot, a player could allow a teammate to dribble behind him. He became the post player who shielded the teammate with the ball from a defender. This play is now known as a *screen* or *pick*. Some modern forwards specialize in setting screens for their teammates. Players soon found they could even post for themselves. By keeping their back to the defender, they act as their own post, keeping the defender from the ball.

Pivoting

The original Celtics performed the first recorded "pivot play," and according to player Dutch Denhert, it happened by accident. "The team we were playing was using a standing guard," Denhert said, "something which has long since gone out of basketball. The guard stood right on his own foul line and never went up court, even when his own team had the ball. During a time out, one of our guys said, 'We'll have to move that guard out of there—he's breaking up our passes when we move to the basket.' I volunteered to stand in front of the guard, explaining that instead of him breaking up our passes, they could pass to me and I could give it back...A couple of minutes later, the standing guard, in an effort to bat the ball out of my hands, moved around to my right side. All I had to do was pivot to my left, take one step, and lay the ball up for a basket."

Today in the NBA, many forwards use the post and pivot plays to score baskets. A forward (or any player with the right skills) "posts up" with his back to the basket. He dribbles and moves until he sees an opening to the hoop, then scores an easy two points.

Guards are known for their outside jump shots. Centers often shoot powerful *slam dunks*. But forwards use a wide range of shots: spin or pivot moves, shots from the high and low post, jumpers from the corner, three-pointers at the top of the key. Lay-ups, hook shots, and finger rolls are all part of the forward's arsenal.

The top scorers among today's forwards are Karl Malone of the Utah Jazz, Bernard King of the Washington Bullets, Charles Barkley of the Philadelphia 76ers, Dominique Wilkins of the Atlanta Hawks, and Chris Mullin of the Golden State Warriors.

Also, because forwards often take shots close to the basket, they are among the most accurate shooters in basketball. Forwards with high field goal percentages include Buck Williams of the Portland Trail Blazers, Kevin Gamble of the Boston Celtics, and Charles Barkley.

Small Forwards

A lot of an NBA team's scoring is done by its small forward. But each small forward has his own unique talents.

Larry Bird of the Celtics is in a class by himself. He redefined the forward position in the 1980s. His ability to make the spectacular pass, get the surprise steal, or make a basket in the closing seconds have made him a living legend.

Chris Mullin is 88 percent from the free-throw line, which makes him the fifth best free-throw shooter in NBA history.

Another forward who specializes in long-distance shooting is Chris Mullin of the Golden State Warriors. Mullin, six-foot, seven-inches, has been called the best pure shooter in the game. He is not fast, but he has a tremendous sense of the game, and knows how to fake an opponent into thinking he will shoot. When the opponent jumps up to block the shot, Mullin simply dribbles around him. Said one NBA scout, "Mullin is an example of how basketball intelligence, combined with a great shooting stroke, can equal a star."

Dominique Wilkins, the six-foot, eight-inch star of the Atlanta Hawks, finds many ways to help his team. Early in his career, he was known as the Human Highlight Film because his great scoring drives were always shown during the sports portion of the nightly news. He once won an NBA Slam Dunk Contest at the All-Star game, but those acrobatics were nothing compared to how he could shake the rim in a game. Wilkins continues to improve by rebounding more and playing better defense. An injury ended his 1991 season and took the hawks out of the playoff picture, but he is still one of the greatest athletes to play the game.

More Great Forwards

Before 1991, Scottie Pippen of the Chicago Bulls was one of Michael Jordan's "supporting cast." But by the time the Bulls won the championship in 1991, Pippen had become a star. His shooting and passing are outstanding, but the real key to Pippen's success is his smothering defense. In the 1991 Finals, Pippen covered Magic Johnson of Los Angeles Lakers like a blanket and was a big part of the Bulls' victory.

In 1984 Larry Bird called Bernard King, then of the New York Knicks, the "best scorer I've ever seen or played against." Less than one year later, King lay on the court writhing in pain with an injured knee. At 29

*Dominique Wilkins missed half the 1991-92 season due to injury,
a trial for a player who loves to soar and score.*

years of age, his brilliant career as one of the NBA's
great scorers seemed over. But King put in long hours of
painful rehabilitation for two years. "I didn't want to
just come back," he said. "I wanted to come back as an
All-Star." In 1991, King was back on top, averaging
more than 28 points a game, third highest in the NBA.

And yes, he made the All-Star team.

One of King's favorite players to watch is James Worthy of the Los Angeles Lakers. Worthy is an All-Star who specializes in post play. Known as "Big Game James," Worthy seemed to have the quickest first step to the basket of any player in the NBA. Many a time he would fly past a defender and finish the play with a creative shot or dunk. In 1988, Worthy was named as the Championship Series MVP after leading the Lakers to victory.

Every team would love to have a player like Detlef Schrempf of the Indiana Pacers. The six-foot, ten-inch Schrempf can play all five positions. He led his team in rebounds in 1991, even though he comes off the bench. A player who comes off the bench to spark his team is often called the "sixth man." In 1991, he won the NBA's Sixth Man Award.

"He does so many things for us," said Bob Hill, coach of the Pacers. "He handles the ball well, takes it to the basket, dishes off, and doesn't turn it over." Of his sixth-man role, Schrempf said, "I don't worry about starting. I just want to get my minutes, help us win, and be in there with the game on the line."

The Detroit Pistons play tough defense, and a big part of that toughness is the wonderful Dennis Rodman. His tough defense slows down scoring guards like Michael Jordan, and he can outrebound stronger, taller centers. Rodman has been named Defensive Player of the Year twice. He is the best rebounding forward playing the game today—perhaps the best rebounding player, period. His 32 rebounds in one 1992 game are the most by any player since the days of Wilt Chamberlain and Bill Russell.

During the 1991-92 season Rodman averaged more than 19 rebounds per game, the first player since Chamberlain in 1972 to accomplish this. In 1961

Bernard King puts it up and over Boston's Kevin McHale. King came back from a career-threatening injury to remain one of the league's highest scorers.

Chamberlain set an NBA record, pulling down 36 percent of his team's rebounds. But Rodman has that beat by a mile, taking 41 percent of Detroit's rebounds.

The Mailman

How can so much talent be in one body? Karl "Mailman" Malone of the Utah Jazz is the picture of what a power forward can be. He's big—six-foot, nine-inches, 256 pounds. He's fast. He never seems to get tired running up and down the court. He is one of the best scorers in the league. He is one of the best rebounders. And he plays with enthusiasm. The Mailman is a hard worker. Between seasons, he spends time improving and perfecting one aspect of his game. For example, one year he worked on his rebounding, and it showed the following season.

When Malone came into the league in 1985, power forward was not a glory position. It was mainly for guys who bumped, pushed, shoved, and did the dirty work. But Malone had skills that were so unique that he brought glamor to the position. He wouldn't just rebound—he would reach into the sky with his huge arms and pull the ball down like plucking a grape. He didn't just score—he slashed through the lane and slammed the ball through the hoop with authority. Never had anybody seen a forward so strong and so fast.

Malone played high school basketball in his native Louisiana, where he led his team to three state championships. In college, he played for Louisiana Tech, where he got the nickname "Mailman." A sportswriter who drove through terrible weather to see Malone play came up with the name, and it stuck. As the "Mailman," Malone always tries to deliver.

As a player for the Jazz, however, Malone was frustrated. Year after year his team would be good. But in the playoffs, the Jazz always made an early exit.

No one delivers the ball to the basket quite like The Mailman: Mr. Karl Malone.

Meanwhile, Malone's personal arch rivals, the Los Angeles Lakers, would win the Western division and go to the finals. In 1990 Malone was irate when A. C. Green, power forward for the Lakers, was voted ahead of him for the NBA All-Star game. Malone responded the next night by scoring 61 points against the Milwaukee Bucks.

"I run the floor, and I'm going to try to put as much pressure on the power forward as I can," Malone said. The power forward isn't the only player who feels Malone's pressure. In the 1991-92 season, Malone's elbow met Detroit guard Isiah Thomas' face. Thomas was forced to leave the game, and his injury required many stitches. Although Malone said it was an accident, the league fined him and suspended him for a game. Malone, however, spends most of his time during a game getting fouled himself (in 1991, he shot more free throws than any other player).

Since joining the Jazz, Malone has become one of the game's greatest forwards. And Malone likes his new home in Utah. "The only way you can get me out of Utah is if you talk, 'Trade Karl,'" said the Mailman. "I'm not leaving Utah. I've laid a foundation here. I have my life on a track that I want it on, and I don't want to get off."

*No forward in the NBA plays better "D" than Dennis Rodman of the
Detroit Pistons.*

Forwards On Defense

The power forward plays defense near the basket. His opponent may not have the ball, but the power forward knows his man could receive a pass at any time. The other team's center dribbles, looking for an open man. The area under the basket is rough. It is called the lane, the paint, or the key.

The next events happen in a flash. The opposing center gets past the power forward's teammate. With the ball, the center cuts to the basket. The power forward sees there is no one between the center and the hoop. He steps in the path of his opponent, getting in position. The two players collide, and the power forward flies backward, landing on his back. The referee blows the whistle. The power forward may be in pain, but he's smiling. The other team's center is called for *charging*. Charging is when a player with the ball runs into another player who has established position. The referee gives the ball to the power forward's team. The forward has done his job.

That's life in the fast lane. Sometimes a forward allows opponents to run into him so he can get the ball back for his team. He may also bump and push for position. When a shot goes up, he turns his back on the player he was guarding to fight for the rebound. When his opponent has the ball, a forward will push, hold, and do everything he can to keep his opponent away from the basket.

Rebounding is one of the most important duties of the forward. While the center occupies the other team's big man, the forward can often go to the basket to catch the missed shot. Physical strength, leaping ability, and knowledge of the game all help the forward to rebound. But the most important skill for rebounding is the ability to get position, a technique known as boxing out.

The forward uses his body and arms like the sides of the box, with the space in front of him being the inside. This imaginary box is the area where a rebound might land. The forward tries to keep his man out of this space so he has a better chance of getting the rebound himself.

One would think that because centers are so tall, they would get most of the rebounds. While many centers do, forwards are often among the leading rebounders. Some of today's best are Detroit's Dennis Rodman, Charles Oakley of the New York Knicks, Otis Thorpe of the Houston Rockets, and Derrick Coleman of the New Jersey Nets.

Traditionally, teams in the NBA have had one forward who could dribble like a guard. This forward

Playing good defense means hard work, like trying to deny James Worthy the baseline.

would do most of the passing and scoring underneath. He would get the attention of the TV cameras, and often got the big salary.

Power Forwards

The other forward was a workhorse, the one that did the rough work. He got rebounds, set screens, kept players away from the basket, and made his teammates look good. Gradually these rough, tough "power" forwards started receiving attention. Dave DeBusschere of the New York Knicks, Paul Silas of the Boston Celtics, and Gus Johnson of the Baltimore Bullets were three of the first important power forwards. They had the ability to turn a game around with strong defense and rebounding. They also got rebounds after their own team missed a shot so that their team had more chances to score.

Soon every team wanted a tough power forward who could battle with the best. Maurice Lucas, Caldwell Jones, and a host of others worked hard for their teams. At the same time, they showed that being rough could also be glamorous.

Power forwards today still play good defense. Many of them lead their teams in rebounds. Each power forward has his own skills that he uses to help his team.

In this day and age, no power forward has defined the position like Utah's Karl Malone. Malone not only has a body-builder's physique and strength, he can also run like a stallion. And he never seems to get tired, even when he plays most of his team's minutes.

Kevin McHale of the Boston Celtics made his mark on offense and defense. The 12-year pro is still one of the most versatile players in the game. He started his career as a sixth man, coming off the bench to give his team a lift. McHale rebounds and blocks shots like a center. He also has an incredible shot selection. He can make almost any type of shot within 15 feet of the basket. Over his career he has made an amazing 56 percent of his shots.

Another forward in the McHale mold is Charles Smith of the Los Angeles Clippers. Smith is a young player who has suffered through a number of injuries. Still, he has shown a great ability to score at will. His low post moves helped him score 52 points in a 1990 game against the Denver Nuggets.

Cleveland Cavalier forward Larry Nance is the type of player who can do it all. At six-feet, ten-inches, Nance is one of the best shot-blocking forwards in the league. Opponents find that he is tough to guard. Nance is too athletic for most power forwards to keep up with,

Veteran forward Tom Chambers had a tough season in 1990-91,
but here he has no problem driving into the lane.

and too big for small forwards to stop.

Tom Chambers of the Phoenix Suns makes his mark by scoring. He squirms through players on his way to the basket, twisting and turning to make his shot. He also has a good shooting touch from distance. Chambers has played in four All-Star games, being named Most Valuable Player of 1987, and winning the All-Star MVP once.

Otis Thorpe of the Houston Rockets has always been regarded as one of the top power forwards in the NBA. His trademark slam dunks, rebounding, and occasional jumpers give his team a lift. But Thorpe really showed his value in the 1990-91 season when All-Star center Hakeem Olajuwon was sidelined with an injury. Thorpe got to play center, power forward, and small forward, giving his team the leadership it needed to keep winning.

Among power forwards, Thorpe's 1990-91 field goal percentage was second only to Buck Williams of the Portland Trail Blazers. Williams is one of the hardest workers in basketball. He rebounds well and plays great pressure defense. Because of his overall defensive skills, Williams was named to the NBA's All-Defensive team.

Michael Jordan and Scottie Pippen grab all the headlines in Chicago, yet the Bulls' Horace Grant was one of the big reasons the Bulls won it all in 1991. Grant plays a steady physical game. He is good at double-teaming the player with the ball, and gets a lot of offensive rebounds. He is also dangerous with the ball, making a high percentage of his shots.

Sir Charles

Whether they play tough defense or offense, the forward position seems to attract big talkers. Larry Bird, Dennis Rodman, Scottie Pippen, and Chuck Person are never at a loss for words. They all have

Portland's Buck Williams is sometimes overshadowed by the dynamic duo of Terry Porter and Clyde Drexler, but his forward play makes the Trail Blazers playoff contenders.

something to say, and they say it often—both on the court and off.

But the leader of lip, the forward that *Sport* magazine dubbed the "round mound of sound," is Charles Barkley of the Philadelphia 76ers. Barkley, six-feet, five-inches, is perhaps the best forward in the NBA today. Although listed as a small forward, he plays a bruising style of basketball. His strength is a lot like the strength of those who play the power position. He is also the most valuable player to his team, often leading them

Come and get it, says Charles Barkley. The outspoken 76ers forward is one of the hardest-working players in the league.

in scoring and rebounds.

However, it's usually Barkley's mouth and actions off the court that get so much attention. He has been known to yell at fans, referees, coaches, and teammates in the heat of a game. Here is a typical Barkley quote: "I have an obligation to myself and God to tell the truth. Honesty, however, is not always appreciated."

What Barkley calls "honesty," some people call "bad manners." Take a certain woman in Philadelphia, for instance. She spoke her feelings in the news about Barkley, saying she thought he was an unkind person. Barkley responded by having dinner with her and bringing her to a 76er game in a limousine. The fan changed her mind.

"If I'm going in on a fast break," says Barkley, "I'm going to try something spectacular...Nobody on the planet earth can guard me." Barkley seems to have the ability to score at will. His size and quickness allow him to get to the basket and slam the ball with conviction. Not only does Barkley score a lot of points—he also makes most of his shots. Barkley was fourth in scoring in 1991, when he averaged 27.6 per game—the second-best of his career.

"Any knucklehead can score. If you take 20 shots a game and make only half of them, you'll have 20 points a game. It's not that hard." But Barkley didn't want to limit his game to scoring. He worked on ball handling and passing. And especially rebounds. He always felt that rebounding was a skill, and that it took more than height to be successful.

"A leader is a guy who goes out and works. There are times I get on my teammates and times I pat them on the back." Barkley joined the 76ers in 1984 after playing in college for Auburn University. He had a weight problem early in his career, but trimmed down to be competitive in the pros. When Julius Erving retired,

*"Nique" Wilkins has long been a favorite of slam dunk enthusiasts
everywhere.*

Barkley assumed the leadership role of his team. Not all his teammates were happy about that. Barkley would yell, complain, and criticize whenever he felt it necessary. Sometimes he told reporters he didn't think the team owners and coaches were making the right decisions. But he always backed it up with effort, performance, and the desire to win.

"I get emotional in the heat of battle. I'm not going to apologize for that." Of course, some of Barkley's desire to win causes friction with players and fans. He was once fined an NBA record $52,000 for getting into a fight with Detroit Piston Bill Laimbeer. If fans cuss at Barkley, Barkley cusses right back.

"Some things I do I wouldn't do again if I had the chance. But those things don't make me a bad person. I'm not a bad person." Barkley does his share of charity work. He wants kids to be serious about education and to stay away from drugs. And he obviously believes in speaking his mind.

"I'm a nice guy who just goes out and works hard at his job. I've done some good and bad things...just like everybody else."

Conclusion

Basketball play demonstrates a contrast in styles. Sometimes it is hard and bruising. Under the basket fighting for rebounds, a forward must be tough and able to take an elbow in the ribs. When he drives through the lane, he dares a center to throw an arm in his way, risking a foul. Or he may be charged with a foul himself.

Sometimes basketball play is swift and graceful. A forward on a fast break dashes for the basket and gets the pass from a guard just as he leaves his feet for the slam dunk. Both styles—the hard and the fast—are fun to watch. And the forward is the player who demonstrates both styles consistently during every exciting game.

Stats

All-Star Forwards*

Year	Player	Pts.
1956	Bob Pettit, St. Louis	25.7
1959	Bob Pettit, St. Louis	29.2
1975	Bob McAdoo, Buffalo	34.5
1981	Julius Erving, Philadelphia	24.6
1984	Larry Bird, Boston	24.2
1985	Larry Bird, Boston	28.7
1986	Larry Bird, Boston	25.8

* Winners of the Podoloff Trophy for Most Valuable Player during the regular season

All-Time Scorers: Forwards*

	Yrs	Games	Pts	Avg
Julius Erving	16	1243	30,026	24.2
Elvin Hayes	16	1303	27,313	21.0
George Gervin	14	1060	26,595	25.1
John Havlicek	16	1270	26,395	20.8
Alex English†	15	1193	25,613	21.5
Rick Barry	14	1020	25,279	24.8
Adrian Dantley†	15	955	23,177	24.3
Elgin Baylor	14	846	23,149	27.4

* Combined NBA-ABA stats
† Still active

NBA Rookies Of The Year: Forwards

Year	Player	Pts.
1953	Don Meineke, Ft. Wayne	10.8
1955	Bob Pettit, Milwaukee	20.4
1956	Maurice Stokes, Rochester	16.8
1957	Tommy Heinsohn, Boston	16.2
1958	Woody Sauldsberry, Philadelphia	12.8
1959	Elgin Baylor, Minneapolis	24.9
1963	Terry Dischinger, Chicago	25.5
1964	Jerry Lucas, Cincinnati	17.7
1966	Rick Barry, San Francisco	25.7
1971	Geoff Petrie, Portland	24.8
1972	Sidney Wicks, Portland	24.5
1973	Bob McAdoo, Buffalo	18.0
1975	Keith Wilkes, Golden State	14.2
1977	Adrian Dantley, Buffalo	20.3
1980	Larry Bird, Boston	21.3
1982	Buck Williams, New Jersey	15.5
1983	Terry Cummings, San Diego	23.7
1987	Chuck Person, Indiana	18.8
1991	Derrick Coleman, New Jersey	18.4

Glossary

ASSIST. A pass that results directly in a basket.

BOX OUT. Putting your body between your opponent and the basket, establishing your position under the backboard and preventing an opposing player from intruding on it.

CHARGING. When a player with the ball runs into another player who has established position.

CENTER. Usually the team's tallest player, the center patrols the area near the basket on both offense and defense.

DEFENSE. Guarding the team that has the ball. The defense tries to keep the offense from scoring.

DOUBLE-TEAM. Using two defensive players to cover one offensive player.

DUNK. To slam or drop the ball into the basket from above the rim.

FOUL. A violation of the rules.

FREE THROW. A penalty shot, worth one point if successful.

FREE-THROW LANE. Also known as the *key* and the *paint*, this is a 19-foot by 16-foot rectangle around the basket, and the best shooting area.

LAY-UP or LAY-IN. A shot usually banked off the backboard from the side of the basket or from in front of the basket.

OPEN MAN. A player without the ball who is in a good position to shoot a basket.

PASS. To move the ball from one player to another.

PIVOT MAN or POST. A player who positions himself near the basket, takes a pass, then pivots to either side while taking a hook shot or throws the ball back to a teammate.

POWER FORWARD. A forward mainly responsible for rebounding, defense, and scoring close to the basket.

REBOUND. To grab the ball off either the offensive backboard or the defensive backboard.

SCREEN. When an offensive player establishes position in front of a defensive player, allowing a teammate to use him as a screen to get free for a shot or drive to the basket.

SMALL FORWARD. A forward mainly responsible for scoring and passing near the basket.

STEAL. To take the ball away from an offensive player.

ZONE DEFENSE. When players are assigned a specific area or zone of the court to defend, rather than covering a particular offensive player. Not legal in the NBA.

Bibliography

Aaseng, Nate. *Basketball: You Are the Coach.* Minneapolis: Lerner Publications, 1983.

Aaseng, Nathan. *Basketball's High Flyers.* Minneapolis: Lerner Publications, 1980.

Anderson, Dave. *The Story of Basketball.* New York: William Morrow, 1988.

Editors of *Sports Illustrated. Sports Illustrated Basketball.* New York: J.B. Lippincott, 1971.

Finney, Shan. *Basketball.* New York: Franklin Watts, 1982.

Hirshberg, Al. *Basketball's Greatest Stars.* New York: G.P. Putnam's Sons, 1963.

Hollander, Zander, ed. *The Complete Handbook of Pro Basketball.* New York: Signet, 1992.

Liss, Howard. *Basketball Talk For Beginners.* New York: Julian Messner, 1970.

Meserole, Mike, ed. *The 1992 Information Please Sports Almanac.* Boston: Houghton Mifflin.

Olney, Ross. *Basketball.* Racine, Wisconsin: Western Publishing, 1975.

Ostler, Scott and Steve Springer. *Winnin' Times*. New York: Macmillan, 1988.

Rainbolt, Richard. *Basketball's Big Men*. Minneapolis: Lerner Publications, 1975.

Riley, Pat. *Showtime*. New York: Warner Books, 1988.

Ryan, Bob. *The Boston Celtics*. New York: Addison-Wesley, 1989.

Siegener, Ray, ed. *The Basketball Skill Book*. New York: Atheneum, 1974.

Sullivan, George. *Winning Basketball*. New York: David McKay, 1976.

Photo Credits

Index